S0-DOO-163

How Can I Find Satisfaction In My Work?

Discovery Series Bible Study

Is there any way that I can find significance in a job that seems to be going nowhere? What if I feel overworked and underappreciated? Do I care too much or not enough about my job? What does God think about my work? Does my job really matter to Him?

These are the kinds of issues that Kurt De Haan, *Our Daily Bread* managing editor, addresses in this study. As you read these pages, you will be encouraged by what the Bible has to say about work and your attitude toward it.

Martin R. De Haan II, President of RBC Ministries

Publisher:	Discovery House Publishers
Editor:	David Sper
Graphic Design:	Alex Soh, Janet Chim, Ineke
Cover Design:	Alex Soh
Series Coordinator / Study Guide:	Bill Crowder, Sim Kay Tee, Ron Busch

This *Discovery Series Bible Study* guide is based on the *Discovery Series* booklet
"How Can I Find Satisfaction In My Work?" (Q0708) from RBC Ministries. The *Discovery
Series* has more than 140 titles on a variety of biblical and Christian-living issues.
These 32-page booklets offer a rich resource of insight for your study of God's Word.
For a catalog of *Discovery Series* booklets, write to us at:
RBC Ministries, PO Box 2222, Grand Rapids, MI 49501-2222
or visit us on the Web at: www.discoveryseries.org

Discovery House Publishers

A member of the RBC Ministries family:
*Our Daily Bread, Day Of Discovery, RBC Radio, Discovery Series,
Soul Journey, Discovery House Music, Sports Spectrum*

ISBN 1-57293-104-3

Scripture quotations are from the New King James Version.
Copyright © 1982 by Thomas Nelson, Inc. Used by permission. All rights reserved.

Copyright © 2003 Discovery House Publishers, Grand Rapids, Michigan

Table Of Contents

THE STRUGGLES OF WORK

Am I Satisfied?

How do you feel about your job? Take a few minutes to evaluate your current situation. Review the last 6 to 12 months (not just the recent exceptionally good or bad days). Think carefully about why you are satisfied or not.

JOB SATISFACTION CHECKLIST

	Very Satisfied +	Somewhat Satisfied + −	Somewhat Dissatisfied − +	Very Dissatisfied −
Hours	❏	❏	❏	❏
Pay/Benefits	❏	❏	❏	❏
Co-workers	❏	❏	❏	❏
Location	❏	❏	❏	❏
Management competence	❏	❏	❏	❏
Relationship with supervisors	❏	❏	❏	❏
Use of skills	❏	❏	❏	❏
Sense of accomplishment	❏	❏	❏	❏
Advancement opportunities	❏	❏	❏	❏
Recognition/respect	❏	❏	❏	❏
Interest level of work	❏	❏	❏	❏
Stress level	❏	❏	❏	❏
Challenge	❏	❏	❏	❏
Skill development	❏	❏	❏	❏
Working conditions	❏	❏	❏	❏
Responsibility	❏	❏	❏	❏
Job security	❏	❏	❏	❏
Other: _____	❏	❏	❏	❏

Review your responses. Are you generally satisfied or not? What would have to change for you to be more content? Are you being realistic about your job or are you expecting more than it can deliver? Do you think you are working at the right place or in the right occupation?

It could be that you love everything about your work—but I doubt it. Nobody's job is perfect. Even in the best of situations you and I have to work with imperfect people in an imperfect system. To top it all off—and this should not be big news to us—we're imperfect too!

If you checked many of the "dissatisfied" boxes on the previous page, the reasons may include these factors: lack of challenge, an irritating boss or co-worker, extreme pressure to produce, low wages, poor working conditions, poor equipment, lack of respect, conflicts over procedures, lack of a sense of accomplishment, job insecurity, too many hours, conscience-violating policies, conflicts with personal or family life, physical exhaustion, emotional exhaustion, poor communication, labor union mismanagement, discrimination, harassment, or favoritism.

Must work be a burden that we have to endure? Does God care about our jobs? Does our faith in the Lord make any difference in the way we work?

Perhaps as you've read down this list you've thought of even more. The problems that so easily come to mind make it painfully obvious that the workplace can be a hotbed of dissatisfaction. But why? And what can we do about it? Must work be a burden that we have to endure? (Eccl. 2:22-23). Does God care about our jobs? Does our faith in the Lord make any difference in the way we work? These questions will be the focus of our attention in the pages that follow.

Labor Pains

The chief executive officer (CEO) of an international firm hired a promising young man, Zach, to fill a newly created position. The work required a loyal, hard-working person who could be trusted to follow company policy in developing a recently released product.

It was soon apparent that the young man, as capable as he was, needed someone to help carry out the company plans. The boss sent an equally competent woman named Dawn to assist him.

As in any new business venture that has to be built from the ground up, the two new employees had to fulfill a wide variety of duties ranging from administrative roles to the smallest details. They enjoyed a great deal of freedom on the job—except for one restriction. They were not to open a specially marked envelope that the boss had put on top of one of the filing cabinets.

One day while Dawn was working by herself, a representative from a rival company dropped by. He noticed the special envelope and asked about it. Dawn told him what she knew. The visitor put on a skeptical expression and made it sound as if the boss was afraid Zach and Dawn might learn more than he wanted them to know. Soon Dawn was convinced that perhaps the boss was withholding vital information from her. She picked up the envelope and peeked inside. What she saw was a real eye-opener. When her co-worker Zach came along, she convinced him to look too.

Later that same day, the CEO showed up for a surprise visit. Somehow he knew what they had done. With tears in his eyes, he said they would be demoted, their pay would be slashed, and they would be relocated to a place where vicious competition and "headaches" would be the norm.

What you have just read parallels closely what happened to Adam and Eve as they worked for God in the Garden. (See Genesis 1 through 3 for what really happened.) In many ways they were like employees. But they, unlike us in our everyday employment, had a perfect job, a perfect boss, and perfect co-workers.

What went wrong? The first two laborers violated the only prohibition in the employee handbook (2:17). They decided to serve themselves instead of the Lord. Their action carried tragic consequences for them and every human since. Included among those results were the labor pains associated with childbirth and the pains of laboring for daily survival in a suddenly hostile world.

> **"Work is a consequence of creation, not the fall;**
> **the fall has aggravated the problems**
> **without destroying its joys." —John R. W. Stott**

God told Adam and Eve, "Cursed is the ground for your sake; in toil you shall eat of it all the days of your life. Both thorns and thistles it shall bring forth for you, and you shall eat the herb of the field. In the sweat of your face you shall eat bread till you return to the ground" (Gen. 3:17-19).

Those obviously weren't comforting words to the parents of humanity. What had been a joy became a process filled with pain. And the "thorns and thistles" were more than simply a problem that farmers would have to face. Every occupation since then has had its own version of annoying weeds that have hindered work and caused pain.

Contrary to the way we may feel sometimes, work itself is not a curse. When we learn to see it properly, we realize that in almost every job there is a way of working for and with God. We need to understand that the perfect life is not a work-free existence. Work was part of the Lord's blueprint for daily life in Paradise.

When we accept God's perspective on work, we will find fulfillment. That perspective includes a new "job description" as found in the Bible. It tells us who it is we report to, what our duties are, and how we will be compensated. It shows us the significance of what we are doing. It also gives us a plan for working through difficulties in our relationships with bosses, co-workers, employees, and customers.

It would be unrealistic for us to expect work to be problem-free. But that does not mean that work has to be joyless drudgery. Jesus Christ died and rose from the grave not only to give us a home in heaven but also to help us to experience a sense of true fulfillment here on earth as we live for Him.

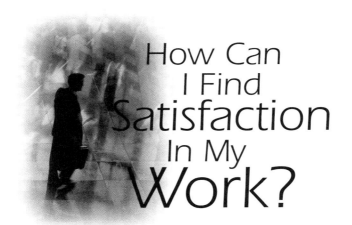

How Can I Find Satisfaction In My Work?

Someone has said, "I like work. I could sit and watch someone do it all day." But most of us don't have that luxury. We can't afford to spend our days lounging at poolside, sipping lemonade, and watching a gardener trim the bushes. Besides, I doubt that many of us would find fulltime inactivity to be satisfying for very long. A Chinese proverb states, "A man grows most tired while standing still."

Our sense of personal worth is closely connected to a feeling that we are accomplishing something purposeful with our lives. Because of that, work and a satisfying life are inseparable. But unfortunately, work doesn't always give us that sense of satisfaction. What should be personally fulfilling is more often a drain on us physically, mentally, spiritually, and emotionally.

If you are a factory worker, an executive, a professional, a single parent juggling two roles, or any other laborer, your struggles are in many ways unique. Yet in many other ways they are similar. This study focuses on the elements we all have in common and offers four principles for helping us to find satisfaction:

1. Know Who You Are Working For
2. Put Your Job To Work For You
3. Keep Work In Its Place
4. Look For A Better Fit

STUDY NO. **1**

The Struggles Of Work

Genesis 2:15—"Then the Lord God took the man and put him in the garden of Eden to tend and keep it."

Objective:
To recognize the universal struggle with work—and how it started.

Bible Memorization:
Genesis 2:15

Read:
"Am I Satisfied?"
"Labor Pains,"
& "How Can I
Find Satisfaction
In My Work?"
pp.4-9

Warming Up
Name five things that give you satisfaction. If you listed them from most satisfying to least satisfying, where would job satisfaction place? Why?

Thinking Through
On page 5, we are given a variety of reasons that we might be dissatisfied with our job. Which ones have you experienced? How has it affected your attitude toward work?

"When we accept God's perspective on work, we will find fulfillment" (p.7) is a bold statement. What do you believe constitutes "God's perspective"? Is that how you currently view your job?

On page 9 we read, "Our sense of personal worth is closely connected to a feeling that we are accomplishing something purposeful with our lives." Do you agree or disagree? Why?

Digging In
Key Text: Genesis 3:17-19
In this passage, what were the consequences of Adam's sin? How did it impact his working life?

What effect on Adam's work experience is implied by the use of the phrase "thorns and thistles" in verse 18? How does this apply to your own experience?

"The sweat of your face" (v.19) implies hard, strenuous labor. How is this kind of labor a curse? In what ways can it also be a blessing?

Going Further
Refer
Compare Adam's work situation in Genesis 1–2 before he sinned with the conditions in Genesis 3 after he sinned. What did his sin cost him, particularly in relationship to his work?

Reflect
Fill out the "Job Satisfaction Checklist" on page 4. Are you generally satisfied or dissatisfied with your work? Why? What are the main factors contributing to your satisfaction or dissatisfaction?

As you begin this series of studies, make a list of specific prayer requests that relate to your work. These could include prayer for your boss or supervisor, co-workers, work environment, tasks, challenges at work, goals for work. Will you commit these to prayer for the course of this study?

"¹⁷Then to Adam He said, 'Because you have heeded the voice of your wife, and have eaten from the tree of which I commanded you, saying, "You shall not eat of it": 'Cursed is the ground for your sake; in toil you shall eat of it all the days of your life. ¹⁸Both thorns and thistles it shall bring forth for you, and you shall eat the herb of the field. ¹⁹In the sweat of your face you shall eat bread till you return to the ground, for out of it you were taken; for dust you are, and to dust you shall return.'"
Genesis 3:17-19

Know Who You Are Working For

During my high school years, I worked for the owner of three small motels on Treasure Island, Florida. Sound like Paradise? It wasn't. I cut grass, trimmed bushes, and pulled more weeds than I care to remember. It was a parttime job, and the pay was low.

One day I figured that I had enough experience pulling stubborn weeds out of gravel parking areas in the Florida heat. So, instead of reporting in for work, I picked up the phone and called my boss. I told him that I wouldn't be coming in. I quit.

After I hung up the phone, I had a feeling that I hadn't done the right thing—then my father found out what I had done, and he confirmed my feelings. I called my boss back and apologized. I also told him that I would work a few more weeks until he could find someone to replace me.

How did I get to the point of quitting that job? As I think back, a number of reasons come to mind. The work was repetitive, the conditions were hot and sweaty, the boss (though not Captain Hook) didn't seem very appreciative, and I didn't see that I was gaining much for my labor—either in money or in personal satisfaction. And besides, I wasn't working to support a family; it was just a job to give me extra spending money.

My motivations for working have changed since those days. Unfortunately, though, my reasons have not always been the best—and I have felt like quitting more than once.

What about you? How is your attitude when the work loses its appeal, the boss seems too critical, co-workers get on your nerves, your family doesn't appreciate how hard you work for them, you don't get the raise you want, and the work becomes boring, repetitive, and seems rather meaningless? When you don't feel that you are getting much for your work, it's hard to keep giving your all, isn't it?

But there is much more to our jobs than what meets the eye. We're not really working for our supervisor at the store, the office, the factory, the construction site, or any other workplace.

Who are we really working for?

Ultimately, we are working for the Lord. He is the boss's Boss, the supervisor's Supervisor, the foreman's Foreman, the manager's Manager. That may be hard to remember as we report to work each day. But if we keep it in mind, our attitude will be transformed.

> **"Unless you can make a connection between what you do all day and what you think God wants you to be doing, you will never find meaning in your work or your relationship with God." —Doug Sherman and William Hendricks**

God is an employer who has our best interests at heart. He's not out to get the most work out of us at the lowest wages. He is concerned about you and me, and He wants to help us in every aspect of our work. The reason He cares about our work—and He cares deeply—is because our actions on the job reflect our inner character and our level of devotion to Him.

We were created to reflect God's nature (Gen. 1:26-27), and we were given abilities to use for His glory. Like Him, we are workers. He worked to create the universe, and Jesus said, "My Father has been working until now, and I have been working" (Jn. 5:17). Man and woman were created to use their hands and their heads to master the earth and make it productive (Gen. 1:28; 2:15-20). Like those first two employees, we are to function in a Godlike way, faithfully working to care for what has been put under our control.

How will this change my attitude toward the people I work with each day?

If we are praying for God's kingdom to come and His will to be done on earth as it is in heaven (Mt. 6:10), then we will be allowing Him to use us as His instruments in carrying out His purposes. Instead of considering ourselves to be victims of our circumstances, pawns of our employer, God wants us to be people of action who positively affect our environment instead of being controlled by it.

> **Instead of considering ourselves
> to be victims of our circumstances,
> pawns of our employer, God wants us
> to be people of action who positively affect
> our environment instead of
> being controlled by it.**

When Jesus summarized the commands of God, He said this: " 'You shall love the Lord your God with all your heart, with all your soul, and with all your mind.' This is the first and great commandment. And the second is like it: 'You shall love your neighbor as yourself.' On these two commandments hang all the Law and the Prophets" (Mt. 22:37-40).

How does what Jesus said apply to work? Love is the giving of ourselves. It seeks the highest good of another person. To love God with all our heart, soul, and mind involves giving to Him everything we have. To love others as ourselves requires that we care as much about the well-being of other people as we do about ourselves. If we apply that to the work situation, it means that our work should be done primarily for God's glory, and that we work with the interests of other people in mind.

Who deserves service "as to the Lord"?

The Bible mentions several types of people who deserve our best efforts because we want to please the Lord. These people include our employer, our family, the poor, and society.

1. Our Employer

As you know all too well, this can be tough to do. According to a story that appeared in *Executives' Digest,* "The instructor at a company-sponsored first-aid course asked one of the workers, 'What's the first thing you would do if you found you had rabies?' The worker immediately answered, 'Bite my supervisor.' "That humorous response reflects a disturbing fact: People often view their boss as an enemy. Developing a good attitude isn't always easy.

In Ephesians 6:5-8, Paul told slaves to respect their masters. Paul wasn't condoning slavery, but those people who found themselves in that situation were to serve their masters as if they were serving Christ Himself. Paul was addressing slaves, remember, not employees who work somewhere by choice. Yet Paul told them to serve with "fear and trembling, in sincerity of heart, as to Christ" (v.5).

Then Paul added some motivation when he said they should do so, "knowing that whatever good anyone does, he will receive the same from the Lord, whether he is a slave or free" (v.8). The ultimate paycheck will come from God. (See also Colossians 3:22-24.)

> **"Whatever you do, do it heartily, as to the Lord and not to men."** —Colossians 3:23

2. Our Family

The Bible also speaks directly to those of us who have a family depending on us for food, clothing, shelter, and much more. In 1 Timothy 5:8 we read, "If anyone does not provide for his own, and especially for those of his own household, he has denied the faith and is worse than an unbeliever." Those are strong words. We have the responsibility to supply the financial needs of our family. That includes our spouse, our children, any dependents, and elderly parents who need special care. If we carelessly or deliberately fail to provide for them, we contradict our faith in Christ.

3. The Poor

The apostle Paul gave these instructions: "He who has been stealing must steal no longer, but must work, doing something useful with his own hands, that he may have something to share with those in need" (Eph. 4:28 NIV). And Proverbs 19:17 states, "He who has pity on the poor lends to the Lord." Just as we are to see ourselves as serving the Lord when we serve our boss and provide for the needs of our family, so too we are to see ourselves as giving to the Lord when we give to the poor.

Another proverb tells us, "The desire of the lazy man kills him, for his hands refuse to labor. He covets greedily all day long, but the righteous gives and does not spare" (21:25-26). Again the contrast is sharp—the lazy man wants more and more for himself, but the godly person is looking for ways that he can give to the poor. (See also Psalm 37:25-26, Acts 20:35, Galatians 2:10, and 1 John 3:17-18.)

4. Society

In addition to what we saw above about supplying the material needs of the poor and our family, we need to work for the spiritual well-being of our boss and co-workers.

> **"The goal of work is not to gain wealth and possessions, but to serve the common good and bring glory to God." —Richard Foster**

In 1 Thessalonians 4:11-12, the author says, "Make it your ambition to lead a quiet life, to mind your own business and to work with your hands, just as we told you, so that your daily life may win the respect of outsiders and so that you will not be dependent on anybody" (NIV). The goal is to win the respect of unbelievers. They need to see that your faith in Christ makes a positive difference in the practical, everyday aspects of your life.

When Paul wrote to Titus, he told him that part of the motive workers should have is to "make the teaching about God our Savior attractive" (2:10 NIV). An honest day's work backs up our profession of faith and points to the truth of the gospel.

In the Old Testament book of Genesis we read about a hard worker and person of integrity named Joseph (Gen. 39–50). As a young man he was sold into slavery by his brothers, and he ended up in Egypt in the service of Pharaoh. It is hard to figure how he could have anything but contempt for his captors. Yet Joseph served loyally, never compromising his faith in God. Pharaoh noticed.

> **"Make it your ambition to lead a quiet life, to mind your own business and to work with your hands, just as we told you, so that your daily life may win the respect of outsiders and so that you will not be dependent on anybody."** —**1 Thessalonians 4:11-12 (NIV)**

Daniel is another Old Testament example of a person whose work reflected well on his faith in the Lord. When Israel was overrun by Babylon and taken into exile, Daniel was forced to serve King Nebuchadnezzar. By the way he devoted himself to his work, his life was a bright light for God in that pagan kingdom.

What more can we do?

Recognizing that we are really working for the Lord is the all-important first step to finding satisfaction on the job. But there's more that God wants us to do. The sections that follow will expand on what we can do to make our work more closely fit the job description that God has written out for our lives. As we do that, our lives will become more purposeful, more meaningful, and more satisfying.

STUDY
NO. 2

Finding Satisfaction (Part 1)

Colossians 3:23—
"Whatever you do, do it heartily, as to the Lord and not to men."

Objective:
To keep the perspective of our work in focus— with our eyes on Christ.

Bible Memorization:
Colossians 3:23

Read:
"Know Who You Are Working For"
pp.12-17

Warming Up

Why do you think God wants us to work? What do we give to God and others when we work? Why is giving to others more satisfying than serving only ourselves?

Thinking Through

"Our actions on the job reflect our inner character and our level of devotion to Him" (p.13). How can you display true character and devotion to God in your job?

Pages 15-16 describe several types of people who "deserve our best efforts because we want to please the Lord." What are these types of people, and why do you think they deserve your best effort?

Consider the examples of Joseph and Daniel in the Old Testament. How does your work experience compare to theirs? In what ways is it different? What are ways you can be a bright light for God in your workplace?

Digging In
Key Text: 1 Thessalonians 4:11-12

Verse 12 says that we are to "walk properly toward those who are outside." Who are these people, and what kind of an effect can your testimony at work have on them?

In verse 11, Paul described three things that make up the "proper walk" of verse 12. What are those three things, and how can they be applied to our work?

How is the concept of working "with your own hands" (v.11) different from self-reliance? How can an attitude of self-reliance lead us into spiritual danger? What is God's answer to self-reliance?

Going Further
Refer
In Ephesians 4:1-3, Paul described some other elements that make up a proper Christian walk. What are those elements, and do they harmonize with those in 1 Thessalonians 4:11-12?

Reflect
How have your actions and attitudes positively affected your work environment? Has your work environment negatively affected your devotion to Christ, inner thoughts, or job performance? How?

How does knowing that you are serving the Lord Jesus Christ and not men help your job performance and your job satisfaction?

"¹¹That you also aspire to lead a quiet life, to mind your own business, and to work with your own hands, as we commanded you, ¹²that you may walk properly toward those who are outside, and that you may lack nothing."
1 Thessalonians 4:11-12

"¹I, therefore, the prisoner of the Lord, beseech you to walk worthy of the calling with which you were called, ²with all lowliness and gentleness, with longsuffering, bearing with one another in love, ³endeavoring to keep the unity of the Spirit in the bond of peace."
Ephesians 4:1-3

Put Your Job To Work For You

What has your job done for you lately? You pour a lot of time and effort into it, but what do you get in return? Have the frustrations, responsibilities, and pressures produced bitterness and despair in you, or have you used the difficulties to help you to become a better worker and a more Christlike person?

As you look back over the time you have been a follower of Christ, you should see evidence of growth and fruitfulness. How has work helped or hindered that process? Do you see progress in your work-related attitudes and actions?

Many of us have compartmentalized our lives to the extent that we do not see how faith in Christ relates to our work. But it does. God not only cares about how we serve Him at church, at home, or in our neighborhood, but He also wants to be involved in every aspect of our workdays. He cares how we make the sale, how we treat the customer, how we respond to the boss, how we work with people, how we handle company property, and how we deal with everyday irritations as well as the major crises. He cares about our choice of career and how well we represent Him on the job. God is concerned about helping us to become better workers in all kinds of situations.

In 2 Timothy 2:15, the apostle Paul wrote to a young follower of Christ, "Be diligent to present yourself approved to God, a worker who does not need to be ashamed." Although those words primarily dealt with the way Timothy taught the truth of God's Word to people who were prone to wander into error, the principle applies to all types of work. We need to strive for excellence, no matter what our job.

Why don't we put our job to work for us?

One reason is that what we are doing doesn't always seem to be all that important. Work can be extremely stressful. We long for some relief. We don't look forward to the first day of the work-week. We often see work as a necessary evil that must be endured until we can punch out and do what we really want to do.

For many years I cleaned an office building in the evenings. That included emptying wastepaper baskets, vacuuming floors, mopping, dusting, and making sinks and toilets spotless. I have to admit that many times I failed to see the eternal value of what I was doing. It was just a job—and not a very glamorous one. But I can remember the times I felt a real satisfaction in cleaning an office or a bathroom. In fact, there are days now that I wish I could have my old job back! What made the difference? My own attitude.

What are the symptoms of the wrong view of work?

Here are a few signs:

- laziness (doing the minimum or wasting time)
- passivity (instead of living out our convictions and standing up for what is right)
- stealing (getting our due whatever it takes)
- grumbling (discontentment)

How can we become better while on the job?

First, we need to view job stress as an opportunity to get better. The trials that James talked about in his brief New Testament letter include all kinds, even job-related ones. He said, "The testing of your faith produces patience. But let patience have its perfect work, that you may be perfect and complete, lacking nothing" (1:3-4). If we encounter a situation that we don't know how to handle, we need to remember what James said, "If any of you lacks wisdom, let him ask of God, . . . and it will be given to him" (v.5).

The apostle Paul said much the same about the value of stressful situations. In his letter to the Roman believers, he mentioned that difficulties produce perseverance, character, and hope (5:3-4). A problem on the job, then, is an opportunity to do what is right and become more godly through it.

Second, we need to realize that even though we don't get the respect and pay we feel we deserve, the Lord will reward faithful work that is done for His sake (Eph. 6:5-8; Col. 3:23-24).

Third, we must keep in mind that it pleases God for us to submit to both good and bad employers. In 1 Peter 2 we read, "Servants, be submissive to your masters with all fear, not only to the good and gentle, but also to the harsh. For this is commendable, if because of conscience toward God one endures grief, suffering wrongfully" (vv.18-19). Peter then reminded us of the supreme example of Jesus Christ, who suffered wrongfully but endured it patiently (v.21).

> **"Masters, give your bondservants what is just**
> **and fair, knowing that you also have**
> **a Master in heaven." —Colossians 4:1**

Fourth, we are to overcome evil with good. Romans 12 contains these instructions: "Repay no one evil for evil. . . . If it is possible, as much as depends on you, live peaceably with all men. . . . Do not be overcome by evil, but overcome evil with good" (vv.17-18,21).

But what if I hate my job?

I sympathize with those who feel as if they are entering a torture chamber every time they report to work. Some jobs are like that, more so because of the kind of people they have to work with than because of the actual work.

If you find yourself in a bad work situation, you have two options: (1) If you are "stuck" because of the job market, you need to make the best of a bad situation, or (2) if you are able, you should look for another job.

Having said that, let's look at 1 Corinthians 7. Paul addressed people in the first-century world of slaves and masters when he said:

> Were you a slave when you were called? Don't let it trouble you— although if you can gain your freedom, do so. For he who was a slave when he was called by the Lord is the Lord's freedman; similarly, he who was a free man when he was called is Christ's slave. You were bought at a price; do not become slaves of men (vv.21-23 NIV).

Paul didn't condone slavery. In fact, he told slaves to do what they legally could to escape it. But to him, slavery or freedom was not the issue. The issue was a person's relationship to Jesus Christ. As we saw earlier, the Bible takes us to a higher level than our immediate supervisor or the board of directors. Ultimately, we serve the Lord, and no matter how good or bad our job situation, we need to please Him by the way we respond to inequities, stress, and personality conflicts.

Ultimately, we serve the Lord, and no matter how good or bad our job situation, we need to please Him by the way we respond to inequities, stress, and personality conflicts.

There is an additional option—look somewhere else for a job. Of course, quitting one place and signing on someplace else could be only a temporary solution. We could really be fleeing from problems that we could help solve; or we could be running from one kind of problem to another. After all, no company is without its faults. So before quitting, consider all the reasons you want to leave. Consider the impact on your family, your church, your community life, your personal integrity, and your relationship with the Lord.

If you are at the point of looking for a job, either because you were laid off (for whatever reason) or because you find yourself in a situation that you equate with "slavery," then the section on "looking for a better fit" may help you think through the difficult choices you face.

Finding Satisfaction (Part 2)

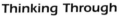

2 Timothy 2:15—"Be diligent to present yourself approved to God, a worker who does not need to be ashamed, rightly dividing the Word of truth."

Objective:
To see the ways that our own attitudes can affect our work.

Bible Memorization:
2 Timothy 2:15

Read:
"Put Your Job To Work For You"
pp.20-23

Warming Up
Is a career in fulltime ministry somehow "holier" and more valuable to God than the work of a cashier in a supermarket checkout line? Why or why not?

Thinking Through
According to page 20, "Many of us have compartmentalized our lives to the extent that we do not see how faith in Christ relates to our work." Is this true of you? Why is it dangerous for a Christian to think like this?

On page 21 we read that one reason we don't put our job to work for us is that "what we are doing doesn't always seem to be all that important." Do you see value in what you do at work? What is it? How will knowing its value help you to enjoy it more?

Consider the four things on pages 21-22 that each of us can do to improve our job satisfaction level. Which one is the most difficult for you? The least difficult? Why?

Digging In
Key Text: Ephesians 6:5-8
To get a promotion or a pay raise in many jobs, an employee has to focus on pleasing the boss. What does this passage say about our motives when we work?

What key phrases in verses 6 and 7 indicate the value that God puts on our work?

What is the promised result (v.8) of doing our work "from the heart" (v.6) and "with goodwill"? (v.7). What do you believe this promise means?

According to this passage, regardless of who we're working for on a human level, who are we really working for? How should this perspective affect our attitudes, actions, and speech on the job?

Going Further
Refer
Paul gave similar instruction to workers in Colossians 3:22-25. How are these sets of instructions similar? How are they different?

Reflect
In what ways have you changed since you started working? How are you a better worker because you are a Christian? How are you a better Christian because of your work?

What are some of the things a co-worker would say about your work ethic? Has anyone at work ever asked you about your faith because of your actions on the job?

"⁵Bondservants, be obedient to those who are your masters according to the flesh, with fear and trembling, in sincerity of heart, as to Christ; ⁶not with eyeservice, as men-pleasers, but as bondservants of Christ, doing the will of God from the heart, ⁷with goodwill doing service, as to the Lord, and not to men, ⁸knowing that whatever good anyone does, he will receive the same from the Lord, whether he is a slave or free."
Ephesians 6:5-8

"²²Bondservants, obey in all things your masters according to the flesh, not with eyeservice, as men-pleasers, but in sincerity of heart, fearing God. ²³And whatever you do, do it heartily, as to the Lord and not to men, ²⁴knowing that from the Lord you will receive the reward of the inheritance; for you serve the Lord Christ. ²⁵But he who does wrong will be repaid for what he has done, and there is no partiality."
Colossians 3:22-25

Keep Work In Its Place

How much of your life is spent working? If you figure an average of 8 hours a day, that's one-third of your day. If you sleep 8 hours, then work takes up half the hours you're awake. And if you consider commuting time, you need to tack on another hour or so each day. Then how about your preparation time and the "unwinding" afterward? It adds up to a big chunk of your life, doesn't it? It's even more when you include the time away from work that you spend thinking about it. If you're a homemaker or a single parent, it may seem as if your entire day is spent on the job.

When it's all added up, for many of us our work is our life—at least in the time and attention we devote to it. Is that bad? The answer to that depends on our needs and our attitude. Even though the amount of time we work can reflect a good or bad attitude toward work, the real issue is not the hours we put in but the reasons for our actions and the kind of people we are on the job.

When does work get out of control?

When we look at work as our primary source of fulfillment and we squeeze out all other interests in life—pushing our personal life, family, friends, church, and community interests into the background—then work has become our god.

The author of Ecclesiastes knew how futile that kind of life can be. He said, "I looked on all the works that my hands had done and on the labor in which I had toiled; and indeed all was vanity and grasping for the wind. There was no profit under the sun" (2:11). Trying to find personal fulfillment in one's work is like pursuing a mirage. Once you've reached your goals you find that the expected sense of satisfaction was just an illusion. There's more to life than grasping for a bigger paycheck, a higher-level job, or a good retirement plan.

Solomon wrote: "What profit has the worker from that in which he labors? have seen the God-given task with which the sons of men are to be occupied. He has made everything beautiful in its time. Also He has put eternity in their hearts except that no one can find out the work that God does from beginning to end. know that nothing is better for them than to rejoice, and to do good in their lives and also that every man should eat and drink and enjoy the good of all his labor— it is the gift of God" (Eccl. 3:9-13).

Ecclesiastes reminds us that life is short, wealth is fleeting, and one's relationship with God and people is more important than any lesser concept of success.

What are the key ideas in those verses? For one thing, although God has put a sense of eternity in our hearts (v.11), we get bogged down in the moment-by-moment activities of life. That can lead to frustration. On the other hand, satisfaction comes to the person who puts his trust in God's sovereign control and then lives responsibly. The author of Ecclesiastes was not advocating a "what will be will be" attitude, a pessimistic and passive resignation to life. We are not merely killing time. Rather, we need to recognize that satisfaction with our work is a "gift of God." A person who lives for the Lord knows that even though life is far from perfect, God is active in our work. And as we trust Him, He will give us satisfaction in the little things of life.

Are we fooling anyone but ourselves?

If you are like me, you may not realize that you are looking to your work to bring happiness. In a recent survey of Americans in which people were asked what was most important in their lives, 40 percent said they valued their relationship with God above all else. In sharp contrast, only 5 percent said the most important thing in their life was to have a job they enjoyed. Some analysts have hailed the results as an indication that Americans are much more religious and less materialistic than they are perceived to be.

But I wonder if an opinion poll really gives us an accurate picture. Who in his right mind would ever say that his job was more important than God? I know I wouldn't. But what do my actions and your actions say about what is more important to us? Don't we all tend to give lip service to God while living for some lesser god—expecting more from work than it can deliver?

Think about your own attitude. When are you happy? What occupies your thoughts? What goals are most important to you?

Am I a workaholic?

A workaholic, like an alcoholic, doesn't easily recognize the real issue. He will usually deny that there is a problem. A workaholic thinks he has his work under control. *I could quit this job any time*, he thinks. But in fact he is driven by his job, motivated by the high he receives from making more money, gaining more power, getting the praise of his boss and co-workers, and outdoing the other guy.

The book of Proverbs, however, tells us, "Do not wear yourself out to get rich; have the wisdom to show restraint" (Prov. 23:4 NIV). If we fail to show restraint, we burn ourselves out—and for what purpose? The author of Ecclesiastes reminded us that life is short, wealth is fleeting, and one's relationship with God and people is more important than any lesser concept of success.

What is the sane alternative?

We need to see the value that God places on our work, and we also need to keep life in balance. We must see work as only one of many important parts of our lives. Don't overdo it nor ignore it. Work is necessary to survival and essential to living out the way God designed us. Work gives us an avenue to fulfill our life's purpose of loving God and loving others as ourselves (Mt. 22:37-40).

Do we work to provide for our needs?

If we are getting too wrapped up in our work, we may be forgetting that ultimately it is the Lord who supplies our needs, not our own efforts. Hard work does not always equal success. In fact, though there is a place for hard work, the Lord is the One who blesses our efforts (Dt. 6:10-12; Prov. 10:4-5,26).

In Matthew 6, Jesus told His followers not to fret about what they would eat or drink, but to seek first God's kingdom; then God would supply their needs. Too often we get things backwards. We pursue the things of life first, thinking that we are the masters of our destinies, the sole providers of what we need to survive. And even though we may give thanks at mealtimes for God's provision, it is all too easy to take the credit ourselves.

> **Even though we may give thanks at mealtimes for God's provision, it is all too easy to take the credit ourselves.**

This is not to say that we should just sit back and wait for God to drop what we need into our laps. God expects us to work. The apostle Paul reminded the believers in Thessalonica that a person who isn't willing to work shouldn't be given food. Paul described his attitude toward work this way:

> For you yourselves know how you ought to follow us, for we were not disorderly among you; nor did we eat anyone's bread free of charge, but worked with labor and toil night and day, that we might not be a burden to any of you, . . . but to make ourselves an example of how you should follow us. For even when we were with you, we commanded you this: If anyone will not work, neither shall he eat (2 Th. 3:7-10).

What areas of life need our attention?

If we are to avoid giving too much or too little attention to our work, we need to recognize the other elements of our life that deserve our time. In the book *Your Work Matters To God* (NavPress), Doug Sherman and William Hendricks mention five parts of life that need our attention. They use the analogy of the sporting event called the pentathlon. In order for an athlete to do well, he must excel in running, swimming, horseback riding, pistol shooting, and fencing. The competitor cannot do well if he focuses on one event at the expense of the others, or if he ignores any event. In a similar way, we must devote effort to five basic areas of life if we are to succeed in living as God desires. The five areas are

1. Our personal life
2. Our family

3. Our church life
4. Our work
5. Our community life

How can we keep these areas of life in proper balance?

Sherman and Hendricks also offer a strategy for keeping work in perspective:

1. "Organize your prayer life around the pentathlon" (p.207). This helps us to remain conscious of all areas, and it solicits God's help to keep it all in proper balance.

2. "Determine how much time you need to spend at work" (p.207). We must set limits on work to keep it from gobbling up all our energy.

3. "Set a come-home time" (p.208). Work tends to expand to fill the time we allot to it.

4. "Schedule nonwork areas just as you would work areas. . . . In our datebooks we need to . . . add family times, church and ministry commitments, community involvements, and personal plans" (p.209).

5. "Guard your use of emotional energy. . . . God never intended for work to become psychological slavery" (pp.209-210).

6. "Maintain a sabbath" (pp.210-211). We need to set aside special times during the week (a day or a special hour of each day) when we can rest, reflect, and put life in perspective.

7. "Cultivate interests and commitments outside of work" (p.211).

8. "Beware of watching instead of doing. . . . There is a real danger to avoid in our leisure, that we not become mere spectators" (p.212).

STUDY
NO. 4

Finding Satisfaction (Part 3)

Proverbs 23:4—"Do not overwork to be rich; because of your own understanding, cease!"

Objective:

To learn principles for a balanced life that include work in the midst of our other priorities.

Bible Memorization:

Proverbs 23:4

Read:

"Keep Work In Its Place" pp.27-31

Warming Up

Identify a time when you were consumed with the pressures and duties of work. How did that experience impact your life? Your family? Your walk with the Lord?

Thinking Through

On page 27, we are warned that work can become our god. What kinds of actions or beliefs can contribute to this imbalance?

According to Sherman and Hendricks (pp.30-31), what are the five parts of life that need our attention if we're to achieve balance? Which of these areas are out of balance in your own life?

On page 31, we have Hendricks' and Sherman's strategy for keeping work in perspective. Which of these eight strategies is the greatest struggle for you? Which one is the most manageable?

Digging In
Key Text: Ecclesiastes 3:9-13

Consider Solomon's statement that God "has made everything beautiful in its time." The word *beautiful* here means "appropriate." What does that say about our priorities and work's place among them?

Solomon said that although we're occupied with the challenges of earthly life (vv.9-10), God has put "eternity in [our] hearts." In what way does that sense of eternity give value to the work we do?

According to Solomon in verses 12-13, what does God want us to do as we think about our work for Him? Which one is the most difficult for you? Which is the easiest? Why?

Going Further
Refer
Compare Ecclesiastes 3:13 with James 1:17, in which there are similar themes. What are those themes, and what do these texts teach us about the character of God?

Reflect
As you consider your own life and work experience, how consistently have you acknowledged the gracious provision of God for you and your family? Spend time in prayer right now acknowledging Him as the source of all the blessings of your life.

Choose one of the eight strategies (listed on page 31) for keeping work in perspective and make a commitment to implement it in your life. Then find someone who will hold you accountable.

"⁹What profit has the worker from that in which he labors? ¹⁰I have seen the God-given task with which the sons of men are to be occupied. ¹¹He has made everything beautiful in its time. Also He has put eternity in their hearts, except that no one can find out the work that God does from beginning to end. ¹²I know that nothing is better for them than to rejoice, and to do good in their lives, ¹³and also that every man should eat and drink and enjoy the good of all his labor—it is the gift of God."
Ecclesiastes 3:9-13

"Every good gift and every perfect gift is from above, and comes down from the Father of lights, with whom there is no variation or shadow of turning."
James 1:17

Look For A Better Fit

"Max" realized that a major change was in the wind. The firm that he worked for was facing a production slowdown. Profits were shrinking, and top management was looking for ways to trim its expenses. Max learned that in the corporate restructuring, his job would be phased out. But because of his years with the company, they would transfer him to another position—a job he wasn't too excited about.

Max took this opportunity to evaluate his options and his future. He learned about a job opening at another firm. The work fit his interests and his training. It didn't require as much time away from his family. He went for an interview, and when the job was offered to him, he took it.

If you, like Max, have the option to choose your career or your place of work, consider yourself fortunate. Most people don't have that kind of opportunity.

As you consider your job choice, beware of the misconception that the highest form of work is what has been called "fulltime Christian work." Being a pastor, a missionary, or working for a Christian ministry is not more sacred to God than "secular" work like selling clothes, programming computers, or driving a truck. All types of work that serve legitimate needs are honorable to God. We please Him most highly when we do our best with the skills He has given us.

If you are at a point of indecision about whether to stay at your current job, or perhaps wondering what career to pursue or job to take, how do you choose?

It usually isn't easy but you can minimize the anxiety. The RBC booklet *How Can I Know What God Wants Me To Do?* offers five steps for discovering what God's will is for you. These steps make up the acrostic G-U-I-D-E:

1. Go To The Lord. Being in a right relationship with God is necessary if you expect Him to help you. You must trust Him, obey Him, and pray.

2. Understand His Principles. What biblical issues apply to your decision?

3. Investigate Your Options. What are your options, the pros and cons, and the consequences of those choices? How do your interests, talents, and weaknesses fit with your job choices? How could you be most effective for the Lord?

4. Discuss It With Others. Talk with people in various professions and also with trusted friends.

5. Express Your Freedom. If you're depending on the Lord, and you've done extensive analysis, move ahead by faith. The Lord will honor you when you honor Him by including Him in the process.

To help you analyze your current situation and the options available to you, use the following outline as a starting point.

Personal background:

- Age
- Education
- Previous work experiences (good and bad)
- Positions held
- Skills
- Interests
- Financial needs

Evaluate job choices:

- Biblical principles (as in this study guide)
- Options
- Counsel of others (family, friends, co-workers)
- What jobs make the best use of the abilities God has given to you?
- In what jobs can you serve the legitimate and worthwhile needs of people?
- Wages/salary and benefits
- Working conditions

STUDY NO. 5

Finding Satisfaction (Part 4)

Psalm 37:5—"Commit your way to the Lord, trust also in Him, and He shall bring it to pass."

Objective:

To recognize the times when a change in your work setting may be necessary.

Bible Memorization:
Psalm 37:5

Read:
"Look For A Better Fit" pp.34-35

Warming Up

Have you experienced a job transition? If so, what was involved? A new employer? A move to a new community? An adjustment of lifestyle? What areas were the easiest, and which were the most difficult?

Thinking Through

When should a person think about leaving a job? In making such a decision, what issues need to be considered? Which issues are the most important?

What are the five steps (G-U-I-D-E) for discovering God's will? (see p.35). If you are in the process of a job transition, have you applied these principles? In what ways?

In past experiences, which of the tools of evaluation of job options (see list on p.35) have you leaned most heavily on? Which have you ignored or left largely unused? Why?

Digging In
Key Text: Psalm 37:3-5

In Psalm 37, David encouraged us to "feed on [the Lord's] faithfulness" (v.3). How has He demonstrated His faithfulness to you in your job, even during the difficult times?

David said to trust in (v.3), delight in (v.4), and commit our way to the Lord (v.5). Is one of these commands more difficult for you than the others? What might you do differently to put these into practice in your life?

In what ways do David's words call us to take our eyes off the current circumstances of life, and to focus our attention on the Lord Himself? What elements of the text help us in that renewed focus?

"³Trust in the Lord, and do good; dwell in the land, and feed on His faithfulness. ⁴Delight yourself also in the Lord, and He shall give you the desires of your heart. ⁵Commit your way to the Lord, trust also in Him, and He shall bring it to pass."
Psalm 37:3-5

Going Further
Refer
How important is it to seek advice when considering a job change? (Prov. 15:22). What are some characteristics of good advice or a good advisor?

"Without counsel, plans go awry, but in the multitude of counselors they are established."
Proverbs 15:22

Reflect
Throughout this study, we have been challenged to examine work and our attitudes about it. How have your own attitudes changed, and how can those changes impact your workplace?

Are there still attitudes about work that need correcting? Does your testimony for Christ need an adjustment? Spend a few moments examining your work-life and commit yourself to please the Lord in whatever you do.

Quit Working!

What if you were hired for a job that you weren't qualified to do? Imagine the stress! Each time you were assigned a task, you would try your best, but your best wouldn't be good enough. Time after time you would fail. You would realize that it was only a matter of time before you were fired.

Imagine something even worse. You've been given the job of trying to live in a way that pleases God. But you're not qualified. You realize that the product of your life is fundamentally flawed. You've made errors of judgment. You often have to admit that you don't know what you're doing. You fear that at the end of your life, when you stand before the Lord, the One who demands perfection, you won't pass final inspection.

> **"For the wages of sin is death,**
> **but the gift of God is eternal life in**
> **Christ Jesus our Lord."** —Romans 6:23

Our lives are that way. We are flawed by what God calls sin. We've violated His laws, His standards of conduct. No matter how hard we work to try to please Him, we can't do it. Romans 3:23 tells us that "all have sinned and fall short of the glory of God." And then the Bible tells us that "the wages of sin is death" (6:23). The only paycheck we deserve at the end of life is God's verdict that we are unsuitable to enter heaven. We don't deserve to go there because we have failed to do what He asked us to do.

But that's not the end of the story. God has done something incredible for us. He offers us everything that we don't deserve. Because Jesus Christ died on the cross to receive the wages we deserved, God offers to reward us on the basis of what Jesus did instead of what we have done.

Romans 4:4-5 says, "Now when a man works, his wages are not credited to him as a gift, but as an obligation. However, to the man who does not work but trusts God who justifies the wicked, his faith is credited as righteousness" (NIV).

Hard to believe? Too wonderful to be true? Believe it—because if you don't you won't have a chance. God guarantees that to be true.

The way to please God is to admit that you deserve the paycheck of spiritual death and to accept the gift that Christ earned for you. By His life, death, and resurrection, He made it possible for you to be forgiven of all your failures, to be credited with Christ's success, to receive eternal life, and to be able to work for God in ways that please Him.

> **It's time to quit trying in your own strength to live a life that's good enough to please God.**

It's time to quit trying in your own strength to live a life that's good enough to please God. It's time to accept the free gift of salvation that the Lord Jesus provided for us. It's time to trust Christ and begin living for Him.

The Terms Of Work

The Fall: When Adam and Eve rebelled against God, the entire creation was infected by the negative effects of sin. One consequence was that work became difficult and full of frustrations.

Fulltime Christian Work: Generally understood to be fulltime employment for a church, missionary society, or parachurch organization. All followers of Christ, however, are to work at all times for the Lord, no matter what their occupation.

Integrity: Consistency of personal character. To be people of integrity on the job means that we fulfill our commitments, that we are honest, and that we are unhypocritical.

Sabbath: Under Old Testament law, this was one day of rest each week. The principle is still appropriate today. We need times of rest not merely to "recharge our batteries" but to draw closer to God and get our lives in proper focus.

Salvation: God's work of rescuing individuals who trust Christ as the One who took their punishment and who offers peace with God. A person is saved not by working hard to earn it but by accepting God's forgiveness as a free gift.

Satisfaction: A sense of fulfillment that comes when we realize that our work pleases the Lord.

Work: The effort to accomplish something; a task or undertaking; a job.

Workaholic: A person who devotes an excessive amount of time and attention to a job, and whose life becomes focused on work to the detriment of family, friends, church, and community.

Discovery Series Bible Study Leader's And User's Guide

Statement Of Purpose

The Discovery Series Bible Study (DSBS) series provides assistance to pastors and leaders in discipling and teaching Christians through the use of RBC Ministries *Discovery Series* booklets. The DSBS series uses the inductive Bible-study method to help Christians understand the Bible more clearly.

Study Helps

Listed at the beginning of each study are the key verse, objective, and memorization verses. These will act as the compass and map for each study.

Some key Bible passages are printed out fully. This will help the students to focus on these passages and to examine and compare the Bible texts more easily—leading to a better understanding of their meanings. Serious students are encouraged to open their own Bible to examine the other Scriptures as well.

How To Use DSBS (for individuals and small groups)

Individuals—Personal Study
- Read the designated pages of the book.
- Carefully consider and answer all the questions.

Small Groups—Bible-Study Discussion
- To maximize the value of the time spent together, each member should do the lesson work prior to the group meeting.
- Recommended discussion time: 45–55 minutes.
- Engage the group in a discussion of the questions, seeking full participation from each of the members.

Overview Of Lessons

Study	Topic	Bible Text	Reading	Questions
1	Struggles Of Work	Gen. 3:17-19	pp.4-9	pp.10-11
2	Finding Satisfaction (Pt. 1)	1 Th. 4:11-12	pp.12-17	pp.18-19
3	Finding Satisfaction (Pt. 2)	Eph. 6:5-8	pp.20-23	pp.24-25
4	Finding Satisfaction (Pt. 3)	Eccl. 3:9-13	pp.27-31	pp.32-33
5	Finding Satisfaction (Pt. 4)	Ps. 37:3-5	pp.34-35	pp.36-37

The DSBS format incorporates a "layered" approach to Bible study that includes four segments. These segments form a series of perspectives that become increasingly more personalized and focused. These segments are:

Warming Up. In this section, a general interest question is used to begin the discussion (in small groups) or "to get the juices flowing" (in personal study). It is intended to begin the process of interaction at the broadest, most general level.

Thinking Through. Here, the student or group is invited to interact with the *Discovery Series* material that has been read. In considering the information and implications of the booklet, these questions help to drive home the critical concepts of that portion of the booklet.

Digging In. Moving away from the *Discovery Series* material, this section isolates a key biblical text from the manuscript and engages the student or group in a brief inductive study of that passage of Scripture. This brings the authority of the Bible into the forefront of the study as we consider its message to our hearts and lives.

Going Further. This final segment contains two parts. In *Refer*, the student or group has the opportunity to test the ideas of the lesson against the rest of the Bible by cross-referencing the text with other verses. In *Reflect*, the student or group is challenged to personally apply the lesson by making a practical response to what has been learned.

Pulpit Sermon Series (for pastors and church leaders)

Although the *Discovery Series Bible Study* is primarily for personal and group study, pastors may want to use this material as the foundation for a series of messages on this important issue. The suggested topics and their corresponding texts are as follows:

Sermon No.	Topic	Text
1	The Struggles Of Work	Gen. 3:17-19
2	Know Who You Are Working For	1 Th. 4:11-12
3	Put Your Job To Work For You	Eph. 6:5-8
4	Keep Work In Its Place	Eccl. 3:9-13
5	Look For A Better Fit	Ps. 37:3-5

Final Thoughts

The DSBS will provide an opportunity for growth and ministry. To internalize the spiritual truths of each study in a variety of environments, the material is arranged to allow for flexibility in the application of the truths discussed.

Whether DSBS is used in small-group Bible studies, adult Sunday school classes, adult Bible fellowships, men's and women's study groups, or church-wide applications, the key to the strength of the discussion will be found in the preparation of each participant. Likewise, the effectiveness of personal and pastoral use of this material will be directly related to the time committed to using this resource.

As you use, teach, or study this material, may you "grow in the grace and knowledge of our Lord and Savior Jesus Christ" (2 Pet. 3:18).

Reflections

Reflections

Reflections

OUR DAILY BREAD

Delivered right to your home!

What could be better than getting *Our Daily Bread?* How about having it delivered directly to your home?

You'll also have the opportunity to receive special offers or Bible-study booklets. And you'll get articles written on timely topics we all face, such as forgiveness and anger.

To order your copy of *Our Daily Bread,* write to us at:

USA: PO Box 2222, Grand Rapids, MI 49501-2222
CANADA: Box 1622, Windsor, ON N9A 6Z7
RBC Web site: www.odb.org/guide

Support for RBC Ministries comes from the gifts of our members and friends. We are not funded or endowed by any group or denomination.

Order more Bible-study guides from these available titles:

◆**Joseph: Overcoming Life's Challenges** (#FSU-ZY507)
   48-page/5-week study on God's faithfulness.

◆**The Lord Is My Shepherd** (#FSU-Z3673)
   48-page/6-week study on Psalm 23.

◆**Jesus' Blueprint For Prayer** (#FSU-H3431)
   40-page/5-week study on The Lord's Prayer.

◆**What Can We Know About The Endtimes?** (#FSU-MW443)
   48-page/6-week study on endtimes prophecy.

◆**Why Would A Good God Allow Suffering?** (#FSU-SK375)
   48-page/6-week study on the problem of suffering.

◆**Does God Want Me Well?** (#FSU-CE513)
   46-page/4-week study on sickness and healing.

◆**Why Did Christ Have To Die?** (#FSU-LZ401)
   44-page/5-week study on Christ's crucifixion.

◆**Did Christ Really Rise From The Dead?** (#FSU-XN702)
   48-page/6-week study on Christ's resurrection.

◆**What If It's True?** (#FSU-L1471)
   44-page/4-week study on the basics of faith.

◆**How Can A Parent Find Peace Of Mind?** (#FSU-F0758)
   50-page/5-week study on parenting.

◆**How Can I Know What God Wants Me To Do?** (#FSU-SM647)
   48-page/5-week study on guidelines for finding God's will.

◆**How Can I Find Satisfaction In My Work?** (#FSU-LY534)
   48-page/5-week study on finding significance in any job.

Minimum order of 10 guides in any combination
$2.95 each ($4.45 CAN)
Plus shipping & handling

Order online at:

www.dhp.org/biblestudyguide/
Credit Card orders call: 1-800-653-8333

Discovery House Publishers
a member of the RBC Ministries family

Box 3566
Grand Rapids MI 49501
fax: 616-957-5741